JUNIOR'S

Parent Guide

DAVE RAMSEY'S
financial peace
JUNIOR

Published by Lampo Press, The Lampo Group, Inc.
Brentwood, Tennessee 37027

TABLE OF CONTENTS

ABOUT DAVE

America's trusted voice on money and business, Dave Ramsey is a personal money-management expert and extremely popular national radio personality. His three *New York Times* best-selling books—*Financial Peace, More Than Enough* and *The Total Money Makeover*—have sold more than six million copies combined.

In 1992, Ramsey founded The Lampo Group, Inc. to provide financial counseling, through various means, to anyone who wants to better understand the principles of proper money management. Twenty years later, the company has grown from a card table in his living room to more than 300 team members and has been voted one of the Best Places to Work in Nashville five times in a row. He runs a multi-million dollar company with a nationally recognized brand, but he defines success by the number of lives changed through his message of hope.

Ramsey offers that life-changing message as host of a nationally syndicated radio program, *The Dave Ramsey Show*, which is heard by 4.5 million listeners each week on more than 500 radio stations throughout the United States. More than one million families have attended *Financial Peace University* classes at their workplace, church, military base, local nonprofit organization, community group or Spanish-speaking organization.

LETTER TO PARENTS

Hey parents! Welcome to *Financial Peace Junior*, our tool set that makes learning about money fun for your kids!

I've been teaching this stuff for more than 20 years. One thing that always breaks my heart, both as a teacher and as a parent, is seeing young adults leave the nest and fall flat on their faces with money. Almost weekly, we see new articles and studies that show how poorly high school kids perform on personal finance exams and how student loan debt has exceeded credit card debt! We've got to change that!

Maybe you think it's impossible to have fun teaching your kids about money. Or, maybe you've decided to teach your child how to handle money because you want him or her to avoid the same money mistakes you've made. That's definitely what motivated my wife, Sharon, and me to start teaching our three kids about money as soon as we could.

In fact, *Financial Peace Junior* is built around the same tools we used to teach our own kids, so we know it works. Your child will learn how to work, give, save and spend—just like he or she will have to do in the "real world."

It sounds simple, but I talk to people every day who wish they had learned how to handle their money before they messed it all up as adults. The commitment you make to teach your children now will set them up to win—maybe even win bigger than you or I have!

We all want our kids to go further than we have, and you're giving your child the tools to get there! Good job, Mom and Dad!

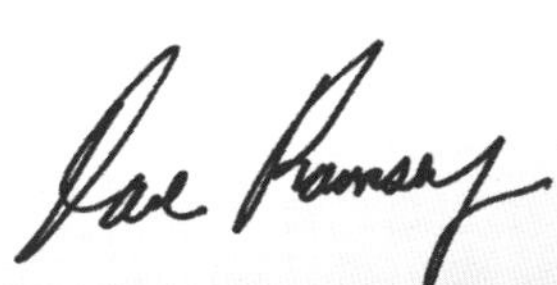

"TRAIN UP A CHILD IN THE WAY HE SHOULD GO, AND WHEN HE IS OLD HE WILL NOT DEPART FROM IT."

Proverbs 22:6 (NKJV)

CHAPTER ONE:
Why This Is Important

Many high-school students enter college and adulthood disabled. They aren't disabled in the literal sense; rather, they simply have no ambition, no drive to win. These kids have had everything done for them, and when they reach adulthood, they are left without the basic skills for survival. Because their parents gave in to every whim and attached no consequences to behavior, these kids have no idea how to operate in the real world.

Did you know that 94% of children learn their money-management skills from their parents? [1] This is why it's important that you prepare them for success. With a little help, you can teach your children to handle the responsibilities of living on their own and managing their finances. That may seem like a daunting task, but you can do it. Even if you are just learning this stuff for yourself, you still have a wealth of knowledge to share with your children. If they see that you are excited about the challenge, they will be too!

You have taken a great first step by purchasing *Financial Peace Junior* to use with your child. The kit covers four basic concepts: working, giving, saving and spending. In their *Junior's Activity Book*, children will learn the importance of each concept and will begin to understand that making money requires hard work and planning. Finally, this *Parent Guide* will show you how to use the tools and components included in the kit. It's important that you read through this guide and familiarize yourself with *Junior's Activity Book*. Working alongside your child will be critical at first. But you will be amazed at how quickly they catch on and how eager they are to work independently.

Even if your financial history hasn't been perfect, you have the opportunity to teach your child to live differently. Congratulations on taking this step, and enjoy the journey ahead!

---

1 MacDonald, Jay. (August 16, 2000). "Our Children Need to Learn Financial Literacy." Retrieved 2011 from the Bankrate website: http://www.bankrate.com/brm/news/special/20000816.asp.

"WHEN MY DAUGHTER RACHEL WAS IN KINDERGARTEN, HER TEACHER ASKED HER WHAT HER DADDY DID FOR A LIVING. SHE ANSWERED, 'HE CUTS UP CREDIT CARDS.'"

—Dave Ramsey

CHAPTER TWO:
What We Teach

Before you begin this exciting experience with your child, it's important that you understand the principles we teach in this kit. Dave uses the mistakes he made with money to teach others how to have financial peace. To successfully teach your child the values of avoiding debt, working, earning a commission, giving, saving and spending, you must understand and embrace these values first. Here are five of the basic principles we teach.

1. ON DEBT

When Dave went through bankruptcy more than 20 years ago, he decided to dig into Scripture to see what God has to say about debt so that he could avoid ever going through that miserable experience again! Over the years, he's also learned from millionaires across the nation, and what he's found is something that few people ever realize: **There is no good debt**. This may seem radical for someone who sees car loans, student loans and credit cards as "normal." But, through experience and research, he discovered that the number-one key to becoming wealthy is to avoid debt. It's that simple.

For more information and resources on how to get out of debt, visit daveramsey.com.

Credit card "rewards," cash-back offers and frequent flier miles entice us so easily that we actually believe *we* are the ones getting a deal. But if you look at the statistics—that cumulatively we have over $800 billion in credit card debt in the United States alone—you can see that we have been fooled.[2] Do you notice who is telling us that

2 Brown, Rachel. (April 18, 2011). "5 U.S. Cities With The Most Credit Card Debt." Retrieved May 12, 2011 from the Investopedia website: http://financialedge.investopedia.com/financial-edge/0411/5-US-Cities-With-The-Most-Credit-Card-Debt.aspx?partner=sfgate.

debt is convenient, rewarding and even necessary? Multi-billion dollar banks and credit card companies! These companies make major profits from the interest that people pay when they spend with credit. Many Americans have accepted the myth that debt is an unavoidable reality, but there is a better way to live: Pay with cash.

Everything we teach in our Financial Peace programs emphasizes paying with cash. Likewise, in this kit, your child will learn to be on a cash system. You will pay him in cash, and he will learn to pay for things that he purchases with cash as well. Although we do not dedicate a lesson in *Junior's Activity Book* to the reasons for using cash, the message of the cash system is woven throughout each piece of the kit.

We also do not discuss the concept of debt in *Junior's Activity Book,* but it is taught in the audio book, *Battle of the Chores* (included in the kit), where Junior discovers that borrowing money is no fun. If your children can grasp this concept early, then as they grow and mature, they can be confident adults equipped to ignore the thousands of credit card offers they will receive. And they will also avoid the number-one money problem plaguing Americans today—debt. One of our favorite mottos is: "Debt is normal. Be weird." And that is what we want for you and your family—weird, debt-free parents raising weird, debt-free children.

AGES & STAGES:

AGES 3-5:

- Understand the concept of debt in terms of owing something back to someone else.
- Listen to the audio book, *Battle of the Chores,* and discuss how Junior not only owes his sister money, but he has to work twice as hard to pay her back.

AGES 6-8:

- Understand debt in relation to credit cards and using money that you do not have.
- Explain why you save and pay cash for things rather than use credit cards or borrow money for them.
- Model the cash-only system for your child.

AGES 9-12:

- Ready to learn a deeper meaning of debt.
- Share Proverbs 22:7: "The rich rules over the poor, and the borrower is the slave of the lender" (NRSV).
- Use credit card and car loan commercials to teach the real consequences of debt.
- Use personal examples to convey the burden that financing and debt cause.

2. ON WORKING AND COMMISSION

Most children learn to spend money through an allowance system given by parents. However, an allowance implies that the child is "allowed" an amount of money just for living and breathing. Although we all love to give to our children, this system doesn't teach them much about real life. In life, if you don't work, you don't get paid. Obviously, as parents, we want to take care of our children's needs and many of their wants, but it's critical that they make the connection between working and making money at an early age. If they are never given the opportunity to earn their own money, chances are they will grow into lazy adults still expecting an "allowance." So, as soon as they begin to understand cause and effect, you can start teaching them the relationship between *work* and *money.*

A better alternative is the commission system. The commission system helps kids make the "work equals money" connection. The way it works is simple. When a child does his chores, he gets paid. When he doesn't do his chores, he isn't paid. This doesn't mean you have to run a boot camp for your children. But it does mean that you are the one responsible for teaching your child the connection between work and money. This is an important life lesson. Teachable moments happen when kids spend and save money that they *earn*, rather than money that they are *allowed.*

You, as the parent, should decide which chores they will be paid for and which ones are expected just because they are members of

AGES & STAGES:

AGES 3-5:

- Respond better to immediate gratification.
- When they complete a chore, celebrate and pay them immediately.
- Help them track their chores on their chore chart.

AGES 6-8:

- Ready to be paid commission on a weekly basis.
- Can check off chores as they complete them.
- Help them add up their commission each week.

AGES 9-12:

- Can manage their own chore chart and add their commission using their calculator.
- Pay commission weekly and praise their accomplishments and growing maturity.
- Encourage them to start their own business, such as mowing lawns or babysitting.

the family. Then, communicate this with your child. Is cleaning her room a commission chore or a family expectation? You set the rule and then stick to it. In general, things like drying the dishes, mowing the yard and vacuuming the house make good chores for earning commission, while things like calling grandma and doing homework are expectations. Children need to understand that some tasks are simply necessary to contribute to the family. Everything cannot be driven by money—a truth that needs to be clear so kids don't expect to get paid for things that are simply a part of life.

As the child grows, the chores and responsibilities should reflect their ability and maturity. Refer to the Age-Appropriate Chores list for ideas. You will also want to take age into consideration when using the commission system. While a younger child will respond better to getting paid immediately for their chores, an older child can be paid weekly—like paydays come in real life. A good guideline to use for paying your children on the commission system is one dollar for each task completed within a week's timeframe. You may want to adjust this based on your budget and the amount of chores your child is responsible for. If a child has ten small tasks, 50 cents for each one might be more appropriate, while one dollar per task would be better for five larger chores.

Refer to the What's In This Kit? section on pages 22-23 to learn where children should place their commission money after each payday.

The ultimate goal of the commission system is that your children begin to understand the connection between work and money. If you can instill a strong work ethic at an early age, it will impact them for the rest of their lives. Give them a taste of the pride and self-worth that comes with a job well done, and they will grow up to be motivated, driven and hardworking adults.

AGE-APPROPRIATE CHORES:

AGES 3-5: Pick up toys; place dirty laundry in basket; dust; make bed; match socks in the clean laundry; help clear the table; set the table with supervision; collect indoor trash cans from around the house; help carry in light groceries.

AGES 6-8: Make bed; feed pets; vacuum; fold laundry with supervision; place laundry in drawers; put away dishes in the dishwasher; bring in the mail; water the plants; sort recycling.

AGES 9-12: Clean windows; help wash car; clean bathroom; rake leaves; wash clothes; put all laundry away; take trash to curb for pickup; help make dinner; pack own lunch.

Children this age can also start their own business in lawn mowing, babysitting or dog walking. They can even stock and sell snacks for your company. Help them brainstorm ideas and learn to set prices, create and print fliers, advertise their new business, manage inventory, collect money, and purchase new stock. You'll be amazed how quickly your child will become a junior entrepreneur!

3. ON GIVING

Before we teach children how to spend or even save money, we should teach them the concept of giving. When we give of our time, talents and money, it develops our character, matures our perspective and creates contentment in our lives. Raising a generous child with a selfless heart should be any parent's goal.

One way to practice giving is by tithing at your church. If you include your child in the practice of tithing, you will instill the value of generosity at an early age. But it's important that they tithe with *their* money. If you hand your child $2 in the church parking lot to place in the offering basket, he won't understand the concept of tithing. He's only acting as a courier, delivering your money to the offering. He has no emotional attachment to that money, because he didn't earn it and won't get the same satisfaction from giving it away. But when children give money that they earn, they feel the pride and gratification from that experience. They begin to appreciate giving as a part of life.

Another way to practice this concept is by giving money to a charity. Perhaps there is a nonprofit organization in your area. Giving money to these organizations teaches your children about the great needs in their community and world. It also provides a teachable moment to explain the need for such organizations. You can use these

AGES & STAGES:

AGES 3-5:
- Will enjoy the act of giving, but they do not need to worry about percentages at this point.
- Allow them to take some money from their GIVE envelope to share each week.
- Help them find ways to give (IDEAS: make cards for children at a local children's hospital or buy a toy for a child in need.)

AGES 6-8:
- Can begin to learn percentages using the easy 10% example.
- Help them add up their commission and figure what 10% of their total is. (Refer to Lesson 2: GIVING in *Junior's Activity Book* for percentage practice exercises.)
- Encourage them to give to your church, a charity or collect food for a shelter.
- Teach them to give of their time by helping serve food at a shelter.

AGES 9-12:
- Can add their commission and figure percentages.
- If you attend church, help them understand why you tithe 10%.
- Help them clean out their closets and toys and donate items to families in need. (Refer to Lesson 2: GIVING in *Junior's Activity Book* for this giving challenge.)

conversations to show your child just how blessed you really are and how important it is to share with others.

You can also practice giving items to a local charity or shelter. One of the activities in *Junior's Activity Book* is for children to go through their closets and clean out clothes or toys that they no longer use. This gives them an opportunity to give to an organization or family in need. When your child experiences giving first-hand, they begin to grasp that it truly does feel better to give than to receive.

4. ON SAVING

We have found that saving money has helped more people get out of debt and stay out of debt than any other strategy. Although saving is proven to work, few people actually practice it. Considering that 7 out of 10 Americans live paycheck to paycheck, it's obvious that people aren't saving like they should. We can't cover life's emergencies, replace our broken-down car or send our kids to college debt free if we don't save money.

Our culture thrives on instant gratification, which makes waiting and saving to pay cash rather than going into debt to have something immediately, difficult at times. It isn't an easy thing to do, but it will reap long-term rewards when you can relax in the freedom of a debt-free life. You want the same for your kids, so help them by teaching them to save.

When your child asks for something, create a teachable moment by talking through what it will take to get it. Show your child the price tag, and help them understand how much or how little the item costs. If the price is a large amount that will take weeks or months for them to earn, give them examples of the amount of time or chores they'll need to earn the money. This creates an opportunity for the child to develop discernment and decision-making skills. They will begin to ask themselves, *Is this video game worth three weeks of chores?* If they decide that they want to work for it and you approve of the purchase, then you can encourage them to save.

We have several saving tools in this kit to help make the process fun. Use the tools that we have included, but also help your children think through decisions. When they understand why we save and what it takes to purchase things, they will become more mature decision-makers with their money.

AGES & STAGES:

AGES 3-5:

- Usually prefer instant gratification to long-term savings goals.
- If they want a big toy, explain that they will have to save for it.
- Tape a picture of the toy to the Savings Goal section on their chore chart.
- Write the total cost and the number of weeks it will take them to save for it.
- Help them to SEE their money grow by placing it in their SAVE envelope.

AGES 6-8:

- May find saving for larger items exciting, but will need help to figure how long they'll need to save.
- Show them how to use the Savings Goal section of their chore chart.
- Help them track their savings each week.

AGES 9-12:

- Talk to them about saving for big things down the road, like a car!
- Praise them each week for long-term saving, as it will often seem like an endless process.

Refer to the What's In This Kit? section of the *Parent Guide* to learn more about the saving tools.

---

3 National Payroll Week 2008. "Getting Paid in America." Survey from the National Payroll Week website: http://www.nationalpayrollweek.com/documents/2008FinalSurveyResults.pdf

5. ON SPENDING

Now, this is the fun part! Spending money is one of the reasons we work hard—so that we can play and enjoy the benefits of our efforts. However, spending money well is a skill just like working, giving and saving, so don't miss this opportunity to guide your children in the right direction.

Many kids fall into the trap (like many adults) of worshiping stuff. It's okay to have some nice stuff—just don't let your nice stuff have you. That means that you and your child shouldn't look for happiness in stuff. If your child is constantly chasing the next best thing to make him happy, he will never be happy. Model contentment for your kids, and show them that their worth is not found in things. After that, have some fun spending the money that you have both worked hard for!

Children can produce long lists of things they want. Some of them you will be okay with, but many of them you will not. Keep in mind that, although your role is to assist them in managing their money, you still have ultimate control. You are the parent, and you make the call on what purchases can be made. Just because your eight-year-old son saves $20, that doesn't mean he can blow it on a movie that you do not approve of. It is good to establish expectations up front with your child and continually communicate them along the way. It's great to give them freedom and responsibility, but you have the final say on how that

AGES & STAGES:

AGES 3-5:

- May be confused the first time they have to give their money in exchange for a toy.
- Prepare them for their purchase by telling them how much they'll have to give to get the toy.
- Praise them for buying something with their very own money!

AGES 6-8:

- Will need help with more detailed spending plans.
- Remind them of upcoming events (like movies or county fairs) and ask them what they want to purchase while there.
- Help them divide their money under different categories for their spending.

AGES 9-12:

- Can create their own spending plan or budget.
- Will be able to make decisions more independently.
- Look for ways to build maturity in their decision-making.
- Begin to talk to them about a budget and how to plan for multiple things at the same time.

freedom is used and responsibility managed.

There are several exercises in *Junior's Activity Book* that will give your child a chance to practice creating a "spending plan." The spending plan is simply an age-appropriate budget. Children will begin to learn how to divide their money under categories and spend within the plan they have created. Help your child create their spending plan, and encourage them by showing them how you create your own budget each month. They will see the importance of having a plan for their spending. It may take some time and practice, but it will make spending more fun. If your child works and saves his money to buy something that he really wants and you approve of, celebrate that! What a great accomplishment!

"A LITTLE BIT OF CONTROLLED PAIN WHEN YOU'RE SIX WILL CHANGE YOUR LIFE WHEN YOU'RE 36."

—Dave Ramsey

CHAPTER THREE:
What's In This Kit?

The components of this kit are designed to work together as a system. When you first introduce *Financial Peace Junior* to your child, it's important to use all of the pieces. It may take a couple of weeks of using the program before you "tweak" it to fit your family, and that's okay. We encourage you to stick with the system's main goals—teaching kids to work, give, save and spend. Below is a list of the kit components and an explanation of how each can be used. Each piece is designed with a purpose and will teach your child in a fun and interactive way.

QUICK-START GUIDE

This flier gives a brief overview of how to begin using *Financial Peace Junior.* It lists the kit components and tells how to use each piece to your advantage. Don't rely solely on the Quick-Start Guide, though! Take the time to read the valuable information included in your *Parent Guide* and review the lessons included in *Junior's Activity Book.* It is here that you will learn how to thoroughly teach your child these life-changing principles.

PARENT GUIDE

As the name indicates, this book is written specifically for you, the parent. This guide is designed to teach you how to teach your child. It provides in-depth information on the principles we teach, and it tells why it is important for your child to understand these concepts. The "Ages & Stages" sidebars will help you know what to expect from your children at each stage of their progress. We also provide suggestions for chores, activities and teachable moments. Don't underestimate the vital role you play in making this fun and effective for your child! Their experience learning money at an early age depends on you. This *Parent Guide* will help you make that happen.

JUNIOR'S ACTIVITY BOOK

Junior and his friends walk children through the four basic goals of money management: working, giving, saving and spending. Whether your child is 3 or 10, he will find something in this book just for him. Each chapter includes fun coloring pages and activities designed to engage younger children. Plus, it has lessons and practice activities to challenge older children who are able to read on their own. Each lesson includes the following:

- **Introduction and Story from Junior** – Introduces the lesson title and tells a story about how Junior learned the principle. These stories are the heart of *Financial Peace Junior*, so it's important that you discuss each one with your child. The goal is that they learn from Junior's experiences and begin to practice the principles from each story. For example, in Lesson Four: SPENDING, Junior works on making a plan to spend his money. After your child reads the story, talk to her about how she can make a plan for her next purchase.
- **How It Works Review** – Teaches children how to apply the lesson using math; also explains which envelope to place their money in.
- **Try This Exercise** – Gives a math word problem for children to solve. Children will help Junior's friend, Dollar Bill, work through a problem using addition, subtraction and multiplication. Includes a hint to help with the math and asks children to write their answers in their workbooks.
- **Wrapping It Up** - Esther reinforces the importance of the lesson and shares a Bible verse for each of the four principles.

Take some time to review your child's activity book before you introduce the kit. You can choose which of the activities and exercises are age-appropriate for your child so that he can fully benefit from the lessons. Younger children (or non-readers) will enjoy the coloring pages and maze activities, but they will need your help working through the actual lessons. Older children (or readers) can complete both the activity pages and lessons on their own, but they will still need you to review each lesson with them. To check their progress, you'll find an answer key in the back of this *Parent Guide* for all of the activities and lessons in *Junior's Activity Book*. But remember, we don't want *Financial Peace Junior* to feel like homework. We want it to be exciting! Spend time working through the lessons with your children, and you will see them gain confidence and maturity as they learn and apply these concepts. And, best of all, they will be excited to practice what they've learned with you!

CHORE CHART

Working for commission teaches personal responsibility. Children will be motivated to work hard because they know that, when payday comes, they are rewarded for their hard work and can buy something they want.

Included in the kit, you'll find a wet-erase chore chart, a wet-erase marker and preprinted chore labels. Use the wet-erase board to keep track of the chores your children complete and how much commission they earn each week. You can use the preprinted chore labels to help younger children associate the image with the chore they are responsible for. Once your child understands his chore list, allow him to track what day(s) of the week he completes each chore by drawing a checkmark using the wet-erase marker. Allow your child to manage their chore chart as much as possible. The more he takes ownership of recording and tracking his work, the more motivated he will be by his progress and want to do more. **But remember, if he doesn't do the work, he doesn't get paid!** At the end of the week, help him tally his commission for payday. (Note: For children under five years of age, we recommend paying them on the spot after a chore is completed.)

You will also notice that there is a section on the Chore Chart for a savings goal. Setting and meeting savings goals is a crucial part of learning to manage money. First, help your children select a reasonable and achievable purchase. It's important that they learn to delay pleasure without having to wait too long to feel that sense of accomplishment. Help them figure out how much they'll need to save each week in order to reach their goal. Fill in the information in the "Savings Goal" section and, for extra motivation, attach a picture on the chart of what they plan to buy. Seeing the picture regularly as they manage their chore chart will help them stay motivated to keep working until they can buy the item.

JUNIOR'S ENVELOPE SYSTEM

When your children are paid their commission, they'll divide it between their GIVE, SAVE and SPEND envelopes.

- **GIVE** – Encourage your child to give by having them set aside 10% of their commission for a church, nonprofit organization or charity. There are several exercises in *Junior's Activity Book* where older children can practice calculating 10% to figure out how much they should give. Use these lessons to reinforce the practice of putting money in their GIVE envelope each week.
- **SAVE** – For many children, saving isn't naturally fun. No one likes delayed gratification, not even adults! But this is an important thing for your child to learn. Use the "Savings Goal" section on your chore chart to make the saving process more tangible for your child. Having a visual goal makes saving fun and worth the work. Your child's particular savings goal will determine how much will need to go into their SAVE envelope each week.
- **SPEND** – After your children place money into their GIVE and SAVE envelopes, the rest can go into their SPEND envelope. Spending money is fun. But, as they will learn in the Spend chapter of *Junior's Activity Book*, spending is more fun when you have a plan. The practice of spending will teach them that once their SPEND envelope is empty, they can't take money from the other envelopes. This will motivate them to make better plans for their money with every purchase.

Many parents ask how much money should go in each envelope. That will vary depending on your family budget and priorities. But, as a general rule, we typically suggest that for a $5 payday, your child put $1 in the GIVE envelope, $2 in the SAVE envelope and $2 in the SPEND envelope. At younger ages, it's more important that they place the money in that order than divide it up perfectly. If you teach them the order—give, save and spend—at a young age, they will begin to establish a habit of managing their money with those priorities.

The envelopes included in this kit are great because they are transparent, allowing the child to see their money grow. They will also feel like a grown-up because they are on the "envelope system" just like Mommy and Daddy. The three envelopes can be clipped together so that your child does not lose them, but they can also be separated for individual use. So your child can disconnect the GIVE envelope to take to church or the SPEND envelope to take to the store. A great idea for young children is to scrunch the dollar bills before putting them in their envelope. Make the money seem as big as possible so that your child sees the envelope getting fuller and associates that gratification with the pride that comes with a job well done.

The envelope system has helped many adults stay on track with cash, and you are getting your child off to a great start by teaching them this method of managing money at such an early age.

CALCULATOR

Kids love anything with buttons, and this colorful calculator will make it fun to figure out how much commission your child has earned each week and how close they are to meeting their savings goals. There are lessons and activities throughout *Junior's Activity Book* that allow them to practice using the calculator. The lessons will help develop their math and money-management skills, but remember that they may need your assistance.

AUDIO BOOK

In our box set of children's books and audio books, *Junior's Adventures*, Junior discovers the values of working, giving, saving, spending, integrity and avoiding debt. In *Financial Peace Junior*, we have included one of those audio books, *Battle of the Chores*. In this

For information on purchasing the other five audio books or *Junior's Adventures* box set of books, visit daveramsey.com/store.

story, Junior discovers the hard way that it is more fun to wait and save cash to buy something later than borrow money to have it now. The audio book also includes an interactive quiz at the end to help your child review what they learned in the story. Your child will love listening to the audio book at home or in the car and learning from Junior's experience.

For more information on purchasing the other five audio books in the Junior's Adventures set, visit daveramsey.com

MAGNETS AND MAGNET FRAME

This sheet of magnets includes a larger magnet frame and five smaller magnets for your refrigerator. You can use the magnet frame to put a picture of your child on the fridge next to their chore chart. It's fun to celebrate them and let them have ownership for the entire *Financial Peace Junior* program.

BONUS MATERIALS WEBSITE

You will find exclusive bonus materials to make *Financial Peace Junior* even more successful for your child at daveramsey.com/jrkit. This site is packed with downloadable and printable activities, chore charts, tools and replacement coloring pages, as well as helpful links and resources.

CHAPTER FOUR:
Keys To Making This Work

MODEL THESE SKILLS

First, remember that your children are watching you. They will model the way you handle money—good or bad. The most important key to making this kit work for your child is to practice the concepts yourself. Then you can show them what you are doing and why you are doing it. If they see Mommy and Daddy working, giving, saving and spending wisely, it will be much easier for them to grasp the concepts. Beyond the kit, their greatest asset is YOU!

BE CONSISTENT

Another key to making this work is to be consistent. Set expectations on the front end. Whatever you agree to as a family is what you stick to. Does your child get paid 50 cents or $1 for folding laundry? Is there a certain day assigned for chores or can they be completed anytime during the week? You don't have to have a strict regimen that has no freedom for change. But if you aren't consistent, you may find that your child is taking the reins and making their own rules. Follow through with whatever you say you will do. Saying "no" isn't always easy. But if they don't hear the word, they will be shocked when they are in the real world and have to make real decisions, like choosing between going to the beach or paying the electricity bill. You want them to make the right choices as an adult, so help them practice the word "no" and make the right choices when they are young.

> **"CHILDREN HAVE NEVER BEEN VERY GOOD AT LISTENING TO THEIR ELDERS, BUT THEY HAVE NEVER FAILED TO IMITATE THEM."**
>
> —James Baldwin

GIVE REWARDS AND INCENTIVES

Learning to handle money well is like any other skill. It takes practice. That's why it's a great idea for you to help your child learn these concepts by giving them incentives and rewarding their progress. You will pay your child on the commission system, but what can you do beyond that to make it exciting, motivating and fun?

A great example would be if your child wants to save up to buy something really expensive, like a bike or a trampoline. A fun way to teach the skill of saving, while still rewarding his progress, is to offer to match his savings, dollar for dollar. This can be extremely motivating for kids because they know that they will reach their goal even sooner. They are still practicing the skill of saving, and they have your support and participation at the same time.

INTERACT

Don't be surprised if learning to handle money is not at the top of your child's priority list. This is why it's so important that you interact with them. This kit is not a toy for you to hand them to figure out on their own. It's a program for you to do with them. They look up to you and learn from you before anyone else, so familiarize yourself with the contents in the kit. Review *Junior's Activity Book* on a regular basis to see how they are doing. Help them make a list of chores. Ask them to help you count money when you pay for something. If you invite your children to participate with you in your own finances, they will begin to gain a mature perspective about life and money.

FIND TEACHABLE MOMENTS

Whether you are using coupons at the grocery store or tithing at church, you can find teachable moments that bring these lessons to life for your child. The more that you relate a circumstance or situation to a lesson, the more fully your child will develop an understanding of how it applies to real life.

Remember, this is a journey and an experience, not a class. Enjoy watching your child learn and grow as you equip them for a lifetime of financial peace.

FOR MORE INFORMATION AND RESOURCES, VISIT DAVERAMSEY.COM.

ACTIVITY BOOK ANSWER KEY

PAGE 3 - TRY THIS

On Saturday, Dollar Bill helped his mom **dust** the furniture in the living room and dining room. He made **$1**. He helped his dad **clean** and organize the garage for **$5**. Then, he helped his mom **carry in groceries** and put them away while she cooked dinner. He made **$2**. How much did Dollar Bill earn that day?

Helpful Hint: Use your calculator to add the total of Dollar Bill's commission.

1	+	5	+	2	=	$ 8
(Dust)		(Clean)		(Carry Groceries)		Dollar Bill's Commission!

PAGE 4 - MAZE

PAGE 6 - WORD SEARCH

I	J	E	N	W	E	C	W	C	E
D	S	K	C	H	A	O	E	P	S
Y	E	E	R	S	Y	O	E	H	N
R	H	R	H	O	E	E	K	C	C
D	T	O	M	S	W	D	N	H	A
N	O	I	S	S	I	M	M	O	C
U	L	N	R	A	E	D	S	R	M
A	C	U	P	W	A	S	H	E	S
L	I	J	C	L	E	A	N	S	A
E	I	S	H	N	H	E	A	O	I

PAGE 11 - TRY THIS

In one week, Dollar Bill made **$12 commission** doing chores and helping with other projects.

Dusting: $1
Putting Away Groceries: $2
Taking Out Trash: $1
Cleaning Garage: $5
Cleaning Bedroom: $2
Washing and Drying Dishes: $1

TOTAL: $12

He is going to **give 10%** to the offering at his church. How much will his total giving be?

Helpful Hint: Use your calculator and multiply Dollar Bill's total **commission** for the week by **10% (.10)** and that's how much Dollar Bill gives.

12 (Total Commission) x .10 (10%) = $ 1.20 Dollar Bill's Giving!

PAGE 12 - PICTURE FIND

PAGE 14 - WORD SEARCH

O	E	D	I	L	N	T	J	T	N
L	S	G	O	G	O	U	H	R	N
U	N	E	N	Y	N	S	E	A	R
F	P	N	S	I	E	I	H	E	E
R	E	E	O	H	P	N	V	H	V
E	O	R	T	E	R	L	O	I	I
E	P	O	L	E	V	N	E	M	G
H	L	U	C	H	U	R	C	H	J
C	E	S	F	O	O	D	E	E	N
O	T	F	N	C	E	V	S	E	T

PAGE 19 - TRY THIS

Dollar Bill is saving for a **$35 toy**—a cool Video Spy Watch! He cut out a picture of the watch from a toy catalog and put it on his chore chart next to his savings goal.

Each week, he makes a **$10 commission** for doing chores and helping around the house. He **gives 10%** of his earnings (**$1**) to the offering at church. Then, he likes to **spend $2** each week on candy or snacks. How much does that leave him for saving each week?

Helpful Hint: Subtract Dollar Bill's giving and spending from his weekly commission.

10	-	1	-	2	=	$ 7
(Commission)		(Giving)		(Spending)		Dollar Bill's Savings!

Finally, if he is saving for a **$35 toy**, how many weeks will he need to save to buy it?

Helpful Hint: Use your calculator and divide **35** by his weekly **savings** (the number you wrote in the blank above). This is how many weeks Dollar Bill will need to save before he can buy the Video Spy Watch.

$35	÷	7	=	5
(Spy Watch Cost)		(Savings)		# of Weeks to Save!

PAGE 20 - PICTURE FIND

Junior has saved a lot of money, but it's hidden in his room. Circle as many dollars and coins as you can find in the picture. Now count the money.

1. How many dollars does Junior have? **12**

2. How many coins? **15**

3. If each of the bills equals $1.00, how much money in dollars does Junior have? $ **12**

4. If each of the coins equals $.25, how much money does he have in coins? $ **3.75**

5. Finally, add the dollar amount plus the coin amount. How much total money does Junior have? $ **15.75**

PAGE 22 - WORD SEARCH

G	E	C	H	O	R	E	S	M	S
G	P	V	N	W	O	R	K	S	J
N	O	I	S	S	I	M	M	O	C
I	L	B	Y	E	N	O	M	S	I
V	E	W	A	Y	U	B	T	T	E
A	V	S	I	P	J	N	O	N	I
S	N	A	L	W	A	Y	S	N	S
E	E	V	E	W	S	I	U	I	I
V	J	E	G	S	W	F	D	M	A
Y	K	E	A	O	I	I	S	A	S

PAGE 27 - TRY THIS

Dollar Bill wants to go to a movie with his friends and decides to make a plan with his money. He's been putting **$5 a week** in his SPEND envelope for **3 weeks**.
How much does Dollar Bill have in his SPEND envelope?
Helpful Hint: Multiply his weekly spending money by the number of weeks he's been saving.

5	x	**3**	=	$ **15**
($ put in SPEND envelope each week)		(# of weeks)		**Dollar Bill's SPEND Money!**

In addition to buying his movie ticket, Dollar Bill wants to buy popcorn, a drink and candy. The **movie ticket costs $6**; **popcorn costs $3**; **a drink costs $2**; and **candy costs $2**.
Helpful Hint: Add the cost of all of the items together.

6	+	**3**	+	**2**	+	**2**	=	$ **13**
(Ticket)		(Popcorn)		(Drink)		(Candy)		**Total Cost!**

Does he have enough in his SPEND envelope for his plan? **Yes**
Helpful Hint: To find out, subtract your Total Cost from his Spend Money.

15	–	**13**	=	$ **2**
(Spend Money)		(Total Cost)		**Extra Spending Money!**

Did you get a positive number? If so, then Dollar Bill has enough money for this spending plan!

PAGE 28 - SPENDING PLAN

For this exercise, simply check your child's math. The items within each envelope should equal the "Envelope Total" when added together. The "Grand Total" should be the total of the three "Envelope Totals" and should not be over $20.

PAGE 30 - WORD SEARCH

S	E	D	I	C	E	D	G	K
W	I	T	E	M	D	V	R	N
O	E	E	O	F	U	N	O	D
N	G	N	I	V	A	S	I	N
K	E	P	O	L	E	V	N	E
Y	B	R	P	U	C	R	U	P
D	U	N	O	E	G	A	J	S
E	Y	P	O	M	E	H	S	A
E	S	E	E	A	B	K	N	H